A Stroll
Through
Life

A Stroll Through

MADDY DANSEREAU

iUniverse, Inc.
Bloomington

A STROLL THROUGH LIFE

iUniverse books may be ordered through booksellers or by contacting:

iUniverse
1663 Liberty Drive
Bloomington, IN 47403
www.iuniverse.com
1-800-Authors (1-800-288-4677)

ISBN: 978-1-4759-9646-3 (sc)
ISBN: 978-1-4759-9647-0 (ebk)

Printed in the United States of America

iUniverse rev. date: 06/22/2013

Table of Contents

Dedication

For all the people who have entered my life from my childhood through the present. You are the ones who have inspired all of my thoughts and feelings. Some of you have brought me great happiness and joy. Some of you have shared your faith with me. Some of you I have been hurt by. Some of you I gave my trust to and that trust was betrayed. But I have tried to be and do my best for you all. I have dealt with it all and gone on with my stroll through life.

God Bless You All

Acknowledgements

To the Keene Sentinel and the International Library of Poetry for previous publications of these poems.

Foreword

As I started out writing this little book of thoughts, poems and verses I was told that I might write a short few words to explain how I came to write this particular story at that time in my life.

The many stories are all true and happened in my life at one time or another.

Some are happy times; some are very angry, hurtful times.

You will meet people that help shape me into the person that I am today, be that good or bad.

I never really had anyone when I was four or five and up that I could go to and talk. This is why I started to put my feelings down on any little piece of paper or even cardboard that I could find. I needed to tell someone. By writing it down I felt that there was someone that cared enough to listen.

The first one happened when I was about four. It is not one of my happier times but it will maybe give you readers an insight as what goes on in my head and heart while I write.

I do hope you enjoy the reading of this little stroll through life with me.

Maddy

A Note from the Author

Some of you are going to buy this book because you will think that you know me. I hope you are in for a surprise.

Some of you will remember me as mother, wife, foster mom, Stepmom, friend or maybe just a casual hi.

I am giving away feelings here that have long been hidden, except on pieces of paper in a folder tucked away from a sometimes hurting world.

I have reached a point in my life where I feel secure and happy enough to share with you all the love, anger, smiles and tears that has made up my life.

I hope you all find enjoyment and a little piece of yourself here.

A Stroll in Life

Come; take a stroll with me, through a world of Green,
For no matter where you look in life this color can be seen.
Many shapes and different shades, Green is all around,
Look for it long enough, a four leaf clover can be found.

Another shade that sometimes twist a man's heart,
The green of the mighty dollar, it can tear his world apart.
God's Green is all around us, forest leaves, plants and grass.
The beauty of the emerald shows a lot of class.

Green of the mountains, the valleys, even in the dell,
the tarnish of copper pennies in a wishing well.
Mint, lime and avocado, dark, light and in between,
I could go on forever, but you get just what I mean.

Peas in a pod, peppers on the vine,
An after dinner mint, a light glass of wine.
Cukes when you peel them, ever so fair,
Still lightly green like an unripened pear.

It may show up in an Irish lassie's eyes,
Could be frosting, paint or dyes.
Spices of Parsley, Oregano and sage,
Mold on a good cheese that's rich with age.

The season of winter so white and divine,
The green of spruce, fir and pine.
The tiny flower buds looking brown and oh so dead,
Needing only God's sun and gentle rain to turn them green instead.

They will all blossom out, just give them room,
Then you will see the Lords work, in full bloom.
A green signal light means you can go,
But watch out for others, move slow.

Some shades will delight you; lift your spirit from strife,
Some will make you want to do more with your life.
I sit some times to see if I can see things grow,
I can't really, but I would like you all to know.

Green is a color, It lives, it breaths,
It shows in the oceans, it shows in the trees.
It's all around us, it's everywhere,
To keep it this beautiful, show that you care.

The Elms, the Maples and the mighty oak,
Could all become ash gray, with one careless stroke.
God entrusted us with His beautiful land,
An uncaring act could destroy what He built with His own hands.

This wonderful place in many shades of Green,
His special gift so blessed and serene.
Enjoy it, take care of it or mind what I say,
He might just take it all back someday.

It did happen once before,
You know.

Memories Not Worth Remembering

What is about man that he needs to,
take all innocents from Gods land?
What is this dark force deep inside,
that sweet pureness he cannot abide?

Children are not put here to hurt and maim.
To steal their souls, leave them in shame.
To live out their lives, hearts broken in two.
To lose their childhood, because of what you do.

Not all men would do this evil deed.
But there are some for it happened to me.
It's been a hard life, both inside and out.
But nothing saved, me not even my shout.

When we were little, we didn't have much.
No big fancy car or house and such.
The place was rented, on a beaten piece of ground.
Shared a drive way with home next door.
It went round and round.

We played well together my brothers and me.
Back then we were innocent you see.
But mom had her drunken card parties,
Loud music, dancing and sometimes a fight.

The boys slept upstairs, under the stairs
I could be found.
On a small cot in a corner, just me and my prayers.

One party night I was scared as could be.
There was a drunken man in the rocking chair,
And he kept looking at me.

He let everybody think he was asleep.
I knew he was just faking.
When a loud crash came from out door,
I was there for the taking.

Everyone else ran quickly outside.
I told him he better leave.
When I tried to run,
He grabbed my nighty sleeve.

Mom and her friends came back way late.
His hand over my mouth,
my childhood was now left to fate.

Crying didn't help me.
They didn't believe me anyway.
I crawled back into my cot,
There was nothing left to say.

I became an angry child.
My temper was to be feared.
I became one on to myself.
Not trusting others and little cheer.

At school I was a loner.
Shying away from everyone.
Working after high school classes.
Didn't know what it was to have fun.

Mother working or drinking.
I stayed as good as I could.
She never worried much about home life,
For she was sure that I would.

The loss of young innocents.
No where can you turn.
Depend only on yourself.
It's a hard lesson to have to learn.

We moved away from that house.
Daddy wasn't with us anymore.
I remember the day, mom took a hatchet,
In a drunken rage chased him out the door.

A baby brother died.
Crib death so they say.
Mom would blame the hospital,
until her dying day.

After mom and dad split,
They started a separate life.
Mom took a new husband.
Dad found himself a good wife.

It was twelve years before again I would tell.
A slap to the face with disbelieve,
And my heart sank to the pits of hell.

Year after year the card games continued.
Each week end drinking would be the same.
More and more players would show up.
Wanting to get into the poker game.

I'd hide upstairs or down cellar.
Any place that I was out of sight.
As I grew, my brothers helped me.
They showed me how to put up a hell of a fight.

Except for the love of my brothers,
I have no good memories to look back on.
As I sometimes think back on it,
I can only wish that it was gone.

One thing I have learned.
Men's evil whims are never nice.
When they listen to their nasty thoughts,
It's the innocent child who pays the price.
May God be there for the innocents.

Home

People are much nicer there.
There's just no way to compare.
I wish I could be back home.
Though this tour has just begun.
It's going to be a lonely one.
I wish I were going back home.
This home that I long for,
Has neither window nor a frame,
It's known as vacation land,
The good old state of Maine.
I wish I could be there,
It's mighty plain to see.
Being this far from home,
Only saddens me.
Life all around me is exciting,
But for me it is all wrong.
I just a country boy,
Maine is where I belong.
Don't think I don't thank you.
You're all as nice as can be.
But the quicker I finish,
Singing this song,
It's back up there for me.
Yeah, people are much nicer there,
No other place can compare.
There's smiling faces everywhere.
I wish I could be back home.

The River

Across the road and down a small hill.
There's this special place.
I can never get my fill.

Under a pine bough is a flat rock.
Water so cold it gives you a shock.

My own private world where I can be free.
A special place where I can be me.

The river so clear you see fish swim by.
Lay on the bank tell your dreams to the sky.

There are no harsh words that make you feel like dirt.
For a while in this quiet world there is no hurt.

After a time it's back up the hill.
I so wanted to stay till' got my fill.

But alas' had to go home,
Until I could return to the river,
alone.

Secret Prayer

I was standing on a hill one windy day,
The world was rather quiet, but I like it that way.

Looking out over the houses below,
Seeing the fields and trees all covered with snow.

Off in the distance some children at play,
Having a grand time on their new Christmas sleigh.

When the moon and stars come out to say "Hello",
Then I might start to walk back home, real slow.

Yes, the world is quiet, or at least for tonight,
So I'll stay a while longer, while the stars are so bright.

Maybe if I say an extra prayer tonight,
The world over will forever stay this peaceful and right.

Questions?

Do you ever smile just for the sake of smiling?
Does your smile make people wonder what it's all about?
Do you smile from your pleasant memories?
Does that smile keep all your troubles out?
Smile because your children love, and your healthy.
Smile because you have the best of friends today.
Tell the world you don't care what life may bring you.
You are unafraid of what it throws your way.
Because your happy living as you are today,
You can handle most anything that's before you,
As a smile will make most hurts go away.
Smile.

Sign of the Times

The heartbreak, the loneliness,
Sorrow and despair.
A great fear of living or dying,
War spread everywhere.

A child that has known no laughter,
Sad eyes never free of tears.
A child of these war wracked countries,
Grows old before its years.

Lay down your arms of combat,
Before it is too late.
Once more fill the world with love,
Instead of this awful hate.

It is the children, who have to suffer,
To save our foolish pride.
So when their world is blown to hell,
Where can these babies hide?

Where can these objects of love go?
When there is only hate everywhere.
How can they grow up to show peace?
When war is all they know.

They die in planes away from home,
Are bombed in their own home town.
Why is it so many have to die?
For a worthless piece of ground.

Lord in all your wisdom,
Your love and tenderness.
Reach down and please some how
Put a stop to the terrible mess.

What are ya up too?

Where ya going?
Where ya been?
Are you asking as a friend?
Why do ask about my life?
Don't you dare to ask your wife?
Where have you been?
Where are you going?
What's the reason for you knowing?
Do I look as though I'm lost?
Do you think I need a boss?
I'm my own boss and the Lord above.
I only answer to those I love.
I don't keep tabs on your time.
You have no right to keep tabs on mine.

Why?

A back stabbing person's life must be
a lonely one indeed.
For a person such as this,
my heart will never bleed.

Wouldn't it be nicer to just close your mouth
and look the other way?
Do you know or even care the hurt you cause,
by the harmful things you say?

To those you speak of,
a kinder gift you couldn't give
than to follow the old rule of
"Live and Let Live".

So before you open your mouth
and say something that is unkind,
know that someone may see into your heart
and see that you are blind.

True your eyes may see the world,
true you may stand straight and tall,
but if you can find no good around you,
aren't you blind after all?

Valentine Love

How do I find the words to tell you?
On this day of days,
Just what you all have meant?
What you will mean to me always.

You are my very sunshine
My laughter and the stars
Up in the sky.

So I just wanted to tell you
On this day of days,
I am so proud you're my children,
I will love you always.

Questions of the Heart

How many times do you try?
How far can your dreams reach?
How long do we hang on to hope?
When you reach out for kindness,
And get back nothing but misery.
I have asked myself over and over,
If a heart can be heard breaking in two?
Feel it bleed and crumble,
When a love has been untrue.
How far away is true happiness?
How much longer need I wait?
How old and tired must I be?
How long do I fight fate?
I know my time will come in life.
I'll have no more fears or fright.
A special love will be mine someday.
He'll come along and with his love
He will make my whole bright,
Because of his love.

First Born

You are my eldest daughter.
You should be the sweetest one.
You're my long awaited first born.
You were not my neatest one.

I've seen patches on your jeans,
Curlers in your hair.
But without your eyes and cheeks done,
You won't go anywhere.

You made me a very young nana.
For this I will thank you dear.
One of my future joys in life,
will be to watch her grow year after year.

Sometimes you do nag a little too much.
At time you're ever so sad and blue.
How I hate to see you unhappy,
It breaks my heart in two.

I wish you always good blessings.
May your every dream come true.
May you find what it is you want from life.
May you find a love someday.
That will be truly true just to you.

All these things I wish for you.
These and so much more.
Along with my heart full of love,
As the first child that I bore.
Love you.
Mom.

The Holy State of Matrimony

So tired of the quarrels, tired of the fights.
Even the sunniest of days seems,
Like the darkest of nights.

Life is barren and unhappy.
It slips by us all so fast.
All our future happiness,
Is shadowed and marred by the past.

They cause so much sadness,
these unimportant things.
Love should be so beautiful.
Not this awful hurting thing.

Why cannot married people be,
happy just to be together?
Why must this blessed union be,
like so much stormy weather?

When you are older, you will look and see,
just where your life went wrong.
You forgot the faith and understanding,
that made your marriage strong.

There is a way to clear up this mess.
Put back the things you took out.
Bring back the love and trust,
Get rid of all lies and doubt.

It will take time to get back,
to where it once began.
To where your life and future,
were on a happy track.

It's worth it.

Mr. Cold Heart

As time passes by you
And your heart of stone.
You're going to know what it's like
To be completely alone.
You give no chance for others,
To cheer you on your way.
You have way too much pride,
To ask anyone to stay.
To help you when you need it.
Cry with you when you are blue.
To do for you the many things,
That people who care would do.
Walk down your path alone,
And when you see the setting sun.
You will wish you had a friend,
With you, even if it's only one.

Miss Foolish Heart

You know he doesn't love you that he never will.
But you have loved him for so long,
And you need him still.
You have given him every chance,
To break your heart in two.
Who's there to shed tears for you?
Only yourself that's who.
You have no one to cheer you.
No one to brighten your day.
Have you no pride at all,
To let him keep treating you this way?
You have done so many things,
No one else would ever do.
You've laughed and you've cried,
Even sang at times.
But through it all you have been true.
How many times have you walked down a lonely path?
Though it's not your will?
Hoping that he will love you one day,
As you love him still.
So watch the sun rise in the morning.
See it set every night.
He will be all yours someday,
For this kind of love is so right.

Silver Skies

Dream on little girl, don't open your eyes.
Just keep pretending, you see silver skies.

He never cared, but you were blind.
Now your awake, only to find,

he played with your heart, he told you his lies.
But just keep on pretending, you see silver skies.

You're lucky you've found how cruel life can be.
Like a lonely harbor at night, or the cold, cold sea.

You'll never forget his love that you lost,
nor will you regret the pride that it cost.

You've loved him in vain, you loved him and lost.
Now his love has grown cold, like the new morning frost.

If your love is true, his you found is not.
You will always keep a very warm spot,

next to your heart which ever tries.
Just keep pretending you see silver skies.

Never look back to, this love you once knew,
for all that it does, is bring memories to you.

The tears that you've cried don't help any more.
All that would help now is him out your door.

He'll love you someday, his kind always do.
Just close your eyes and look to the blue.
He'll want you back; though you know it's wrong,
he'll start to win you with his old sweet song,

Of lies and fables which never can be,
but you'll be alone again, don't you see?

That if all that he offers is fables and lies.
Then that's what you want though part of you dies.

It really doesn't matter the times that you'll cry,
for you know that without him, there is no silver skies.

What Men Really Want in a Wife

A gourmet cook in the kitchen.
A puritan at home, when company comes.
A sexy siren in the bedroom,
When the rest of the house work is done.
A handy helper at all odd jobs.
But Lord, don't ever offer her advice.
Always make him feel the smartest,
now wouldn't that be nice?
A job to help with household expenses,
but never talk about it, unless you are alone.
For when things are running smoothly.
He likes to feel he's done it on his own.
Well most times he is there when you need him.
With tenderness, understanding and love.
When after twenty five years,
You can both smile at each other.
You can still walk hand in hand,
"That is Love"!!!

Homer

If happiness could ever be measured,
I couldn't find a big enough cup.

When I'm down and feeling empty,
your love for me fills me up.

Just to reach out in the night to touch you,
means more to me than words can say.

For your nearness when I need you,
to take all my sadness away.

I don't always say it as I feel it,
but one thing I want you to know.

My trust and love for you are forever.
Our future ahead will only grow.

I will always be honest and faithful.
I fully expect the same of you.

For without these things in our lives,
a marriage would be fake and untrue.

It may fool the world on the outside,
may even fool ourselves for a while.

There is hurt and tears that show,
that can never be covered with a smile.

Marriage is a lot of hard work.
Working together we can build it up.

Side by side we can do it,
and in years to come fill both our cups.

Together.

Not Losing a Dad

Somewhere in the wind please remember me.
Some place in time could you remember you cared.
In your other world, I was just a boy.
Your boy.
I am your son.
I wasted your time.
I wasted my youth.
I wanted everything today.
I wanted all of it yesterday.
I was meant to be mine. Then "she" came.
I was no longer the youngest, the "one".
I really tried to hate her.
I didn't want her here.
Her baby was the" one" now.
Younger than me and a GIRL.
She kept the house clean.
She could really cook.
My socks matched.
I just didn't want her in my dad's life.
What do I say to a son that thinks I don't understand?
How do I say "it's O.K. to cry"?
When at twelve, he wants so bad to be a man
Will I ever get the chance to tell you "I love you"?
I didn't send your mother away.
Your dad loves me and I love him,
From now on it's going to be that way.
Can we not at least be,
Friends?

Boys Do Cry and It's OK

What do you say to a boy, who thinks,
you just don't understand.
How do you say it's o.k. to cry?
When he wants so bad to be a man.
Will I ever get a chance to tell him?
Will I ever get the chance to say?
I'm not trying to replace your mother.
I'm not trying to take your father away.
I'm here to love you all that I can.
To guide you a little as you grow.
I know you are bewildered and unhappy.
I know you sometimes feel miserable and blue.
With your mom walking out of your life as she did.
You need and want more love from your dad.
I do love your dad dearly.
This fact I want you to know.
I don't wish to run your life.
But it would be so nice to share it.
Because we both do love your dad.
Do you think that you can bear it?
In a wink of a parents eye you kids,
will all be gone from home.
As you all take that first worldly step.
As you move further away.
How many times will you really look back?
And say "l wonder if the folks are O.K"?
So dear son, as you start into life on your own,
Do you really want to see your dad alone????
I pray not.

Smiles

What can smiles do?
Oh so many things.
Bring tears of joy and laughter,
Maybe even a wedding ring.
Take the gray sky,
Turn it to blue and sunny.
Won't cure a heartache,
Won't hurt to try.
A smile can make an old man,
Feel like a young boy.
Take some sadness,
Turn it to joy.
A smile will not turn the world upside down.
It makes your life better than a frown.
So lift a heart,
Give sunshine away.
Greet the people you meet
With a smile today.

1st Infantry Division U.S.A.

A million miles away from home,
somewhere across the sea.
Are the duty bound army men
of the fighting first infantry.

They left their loved ones here behind.
To fight a good cause, I guess.
When "Uncle Sugar" called these men,
he's called the very best.

No mission is too difficult.
No sacrifice is too great.
If it isn't considered a duty,
Sorry! It will have to wait.

They've learned to spit and polish.
They've learned to press shirts and pants.
They have learned to fight with the best,
To protect those that can't.

There are times when they are lonely.
There are others when they are blue.
Please don't think, for a minute fellows,
our hearts and prayers are not there with you.

He was my son, for him it's over now.
He's gone on high to heal and rest.
He gave his all for his country.
while fighting with the best.

For the fine job that you all are doing.
Thank you for your sacrifice and pain.
God's world will know peace someday,
with faith this won't all be in vain.

We Pray! My Middle Love

As you start into your adult life,
Not knowing what it has in store.
May it always be just happiness and more.
You have been such a joy to me,
As I now look back.
The many, many time you made me smile,
I had somehow lost track.

Shy and quiet as a tot.
With a heart so full of love.
I knew the moment I held you,
I was surely blessed from above.

Now as you go from ribbons to curlers.
From jeans to someday a wedding dress.
Remember what I've tried to teach you.
Life can so easily become a mess.

I don't ever want you unhappy.
Never see you sad or blue.
But should tears come and you need comfort,
please know that I am here and I love you.

I'm proud of you as you are dear.
Proud of you I will always be.
I have loved you as your own person.
Thank God you did the same with me.

Mothers Child

Some shout. Some scold. Some spank.
When they should be on their knees in thanks.

Thanks for that love that will never fade.
Though your hair will grow to that grayer shade.

A child is to love to hold and to cheer.
To guide and get better year after year.

Love your children. *Don't* make them cry.
It's sad to see sad tears in their eyes.

Who needs riches of silver and gold?
What use will it be when you are old?

Give those hugs and kisses day and night.
It is sure to make everything alright.

Thank the Lord for their love.
Never let them feel their alone.

In the future no matter where they roam,
they'll always have good memories of home.

When they are happy and settled,
then you can look back with a smile.

You and the Lord did a good job,
though you were lost for a while.

Second Family Arnold & Lera

Two of the nicest people in this world.
Tell me I remind them of their little girl.

She left this world when she was a child.
It was a long, long time before they could smile.

There is no broken heart, like that of a mother.
When she finds out she cannot have another.

They were aunt and uncle to friends of mine.
We went to a wedding, stood in that line.

When our turn came they met us graciously.
From then on they adopted my family and me.

Picnics and lunches exchanged back and forth.
Chit chat for hours, who could ask for more.

Whenever we needed a helping hand.
They were always there, it was grand.

Aside from the help, knowing they were there,
Whenever we see them they showed their care.

With laughter and love all around.
Nowhere will sweeter people be found.

Someday they may need help from me.
Love and that help will be given willingly.

Sweet Happy Sixteen

I don't know what other girls are made of.
But I think I know my daughter well.
Bashful and shy as a little tot,
as she grew she came out of her shell.

With a heart big as the moon, being saved
for that special guy.
With giggles, laughter and sunshine or
So sad it makes me want to cry.

I've no dream of seeing you president.
Or queen in some far off land.
To see you happy as you grow
Your dreams realized would be grand.

I'll try to always be there for you
when life seems all up hill.
To show that I love you dear
and that I always will.

There is no need for presents, mom
nor any of those other frills.
Just knowing that your there for me
that's my birthday thrill.

So have a happy birthday daughter of mine
with this gift I cannot wrap.
My love forever and always
Shopping for this gift was a snap.

I had it within me all along.

Love mom

Hurtful Secrets

The sorrow they brings,
such hurt they bestow
not to be trusted
with the truth anymore.
Someone dear has died.
His body buried last fall.
Disease has taken another.
His sweet soul, gone without,
even a polite call.
Don't tell them about this.
Keep it hidden away.
Just say he went in peace.
Keep the truth hidden,
it's better that way.
Well-meant intentions are
the most hurtful kind.
Not to see the loss of weight,
the pain etched in his face.
They knew I wasn't blind.
I tried to go see him.
His family said let him be.
But I'm his friend, so are others,
He'll want to see me.
Too some he's like a brother.
They feared that someone would hear,
that he had the dreaded Aids,
they were living in cowardly fear.

They worried about themselves.
Afraid the world would turn its back.
Alone! They let him die alone.
They thought no one would care.
Had they called his friends
we'd have all been there.
Why the lies?
What's with the secrets?
Why did my friend have to die this way?
Thinking that his friends didn't care.
Secrets are such hurtful things.
Maybe we will understand,
someday.

Snow, the Beauty of It

Try to imagine, what it would be like,
If snow were any other color but White.
Think of everything as one shade of Red,
Then again Brown would make all things seem dead.
Black would leave us in the dark of night,
Purple would give us all a fright.
Orange or Yellow pretty for a dress,
But to cover the world would be a mess.
Think of all around you, as shades of blue,
In a very short time, you would be to.
But the Lord in his wisdom was very smart,
He knew that White was the right color from the start.

Work Day

Why go to work to moan and groan?
Just give up and stay at home.
To work with ease grace and a smile,
will always make your day worthwhile.

Hello, good morning,
how are you today?
With a smile always handy,
work just flows away.

There is good in others,
look hard you will see.
I ask you now, "What's wrong,
with working cheerfully?"

Be good to your coworkers,
lend them all hand.
Then when you need it
they will help you when they can.

If you just go to work
just to moan and groan.
Do everyone a favor,
stay at home by yourself alone.

Something Special Inside

Some people smile though they are sad.
Some people cry even when their glad.
Just to walk down the street,
And be able to say,
To the people around you,
"What a wonderful day".
I wish something like this could happen to me.
But it's just my dream, for you see,
I have Muscular Dystrophy.
I am getting all the help that I can.
I want to help others when I'm a man.
So please don't cry for me.
Send me a card of good cheer.
Maybe . . . just maybe,
I will be better next year.

Questions of the Heart

How many times do you try?
How far can your dreams reach?
How long do we hang on to hope?
When you reach out for kindness,
And get back nothing but misery.
I have asked myself over and over,
If a heart can be heard breaking in two?
Feel it bleed and crumble,
When a love has been untrue.
How far away is true happiness?
How much longer need I wait?
How old and tired must I be?
How long do I fight fate?
I know my time will come in life.
I'll have no more fears or fright.
A special love will be mine someday.
He'll come along and with his love
He will make my whole bright,
Because of his love.

I Am As I Say

Until I lose your respect through an act of my own,
do not hold it from me.

Until I deserve it by provoking it,
Do not show me anger.

Because I show kindness and understanding,
Do not think of me as simple or a fool.

When I offer help, it's because I care.
Not because I think I know it all.

When I offer love,
don't hold yours from me for pettiness and spite.

When I stumble,
help me do not laugh at me.

When I am in darkness, hold a light.
Don't close another door.

I will try to be what you want me to be.
I will be the kind of friend you deserve.

I will sometimes fail you,
but not by choice.

I will make mistakes.
I am not God.

Do not judge me.
You are not Him either.

Walk beside me,
not above me.

Given respect,
I will give it wholeheartedly.

Given anger,
I will return it tenfold.

Given kindness and love,
I will show it also.

Help me with understanding,
I will do the same for you.

I am my own person.
I know who and what I am.

I know just where I am going.
I may change my ways for you.

I will not tolerate you trying to change me.
I will not be walked upon or used.

I will fight back.

A Boy Named John

Her own first party,
Excitement is high.
It's a surprise for her
Special guy.

Run to the store.
More soda and chips.
Back to the store again,
Forgot the dips.

Times getting closer and
Closer at hand.
When out the window
She sees her man.

She jumps and giggles,
Runs through the house.
He's inside now,
she's quiet as a mouse.

The cakes have been cut.
Soda is gone.
Her first party a success,
For her boyfriend John.

Friends Gone Astray

There's no doubt your love is true.
It's written in your eyes.
Between you no words are needed,
It's all said with tender sighs.

Seeing you two together ever so content.
Knowing you both feel what you have,
has been heaven sent.

At times you're like a couple of kids,
playing at the game of romance.
For all the shame and hurt it could cause,
do you really think it's worth the chance?

It's said that real true love,
comes but once in your life.
The hell is going to really start,
when it's with another man's wife.

You could be with someone who's free to love you.
You know that you really should.
You tell yourself you can't live without her.
Trying to make yourself feel good.

Take happiness as you find it,
Is some people's outlook in life.
Why try to take that happiness,
by causing someone else strife.

Before you get any deeper.
Be sure this is for you.
If she cheats on the one she's with now,
can you be sure she'll ever be true?

Some people say don't look back,
but you will learn from your mistakes.
No one's peace of mind ever comes,
From someone else's heartache.

Oh, I know it's none of my business.
You can tell me that if you wanted to.
I'm not saying these things to hurt.
I'm saying them only because I care for you.

So friend be sure of what you're getting into.
Heartache is headed your way.
When she walks away "and she will",
For your own good, don't ask her to stay.

Vally of Sinners

I walk through the valley of sinners.
I walk there unafraid.
For I have the hand of Jesus,
To guide me on my way

Though I walk in that valley of sinners,
of heartbreak and dishonesty.
I have no great fear of falling,
for Jesus is watching over me.

If you fall to that valley of lost souls,
say a prayer and walk on through.
Stand straight and tall with the Lord,
His love is waiting there for you.

Give your faith to God above.
He gives back all His love.
Just follow His guiding light
Early morn too late at night.
He will take your fears away.
You will never want to stray.

Yes we all walk the valley of sinners,
in this world of heartbreak and dishonesty.
But have no fear of falling,
The Lord is watching over you and me.

One More Heart Free

Die heart.
Cry heart.
Bleed some more for me.
Don't fight it heart.
Just break heart.
God, knows he won't set you free.

What's the matter heart?
You're not crying heart.
You didn't shed one tear today.

Keep going now, oh!
don't look back
now you're on your way.

You are breaking free of things,
that took hold of you.
That thing that some fools
may call love.

No need to cry heart.
No need to die heart.
The bleeding soon will stop.

Pick up the pieces.
Start over.
Try again.

Don't trust!
Don't dream!
Don't love!

Play it smart!!!
It is over.

Chosen Child

I'd like to see the beauty of this land.
I'd like to have a fellow hold my hand.
I can hear the sound of spring, summer and fall.
I can smell the cleanness and freshness of it all.
To look to the sky and the birds that fly.
To see this world once I would gladly die.
Just to look in the mirror to see how to dress,
or know by sight that my hair not a mess.
To know that someday I'd have a child of my own.
Have a loving husband that wouldn't leave me alone.
But the Lord wanted a child that could not see.
So I understand now why He choose me.
I'm special!!

Where a Mothers Heart lies

God lent to me eight precious jewels,
Each one a priceless gem.
Because of the trust He's shown in me
I will always be thankful to Him.
I will do my very best to love and care
for them, to see that they grow right.
Oh! There will be some sadness, joy
and some sorrow.
But lots and lots of happiness, in their
future tomorrows.
They'll be mine for such a short time.
They'll grow, marry and leave me alone.
May they not forget the lessons of home.
Build their lives with understanding,
tenderness and love.
Give a happy life for all you care for,
And receive the Lord's blessings from above.

Proud All American Woman

I'm neither debonair nor sophisticated.
I'm not petite, dimpled nor sweet.
Though I do love you dearly,
don't wipe upon me your feet.

Oh yes I'm bold brassy and mouthy,
at times a little too crude.
Try to remember at all times,
my love is long lasting and true.

So . . . honey just you bear with me.
Try your very best to understand.
Accept my faults as I do yours,
I'll be the very best wife that I can.

Golf Widows Surrender

It's spring again and the fever has hit.
Best be careful now or you'll be struck by it.

Time for the knee knocker pants and cute beanie hats.
No other time in your life would you dress like that.

As you try to improve on your stroke and save your pride. Sorry!
But family, business and friends need to step aside.

You lift enough weight to break your back.
Carrying cute little iron clubs in a sack.

You chase tiny balls to and fro.
Then stand on the 'green' and ask where did it go?

Caught in a sand trap or a lily pond.
If no one is looking, get a new ball and move on.

Neither one hundred degree sun or freezing rain,
will stop all your fun and think about going again.

Now at home after a long day at play.
It's all you talk about until the next golf day.

Course you could be out drinking, or chasing skirts of all sorts.
So go ahead honey chase that cute little ball for a sport.

"Chubby"

There is this fellow we work with.
Who is really quite a man.
Though you wouldn't know it to look at him.
He is a lover of the land.

When the white stuff starts falling.
He really prays and hopes.
That he can get away for the weekend from work,
to all those sweet curves and slopes.

On the shady side of thirty.
He cut quite a figure in his day.
He's tackle a biggest mogul around.
Not missing a jump on the way.

A far away look when he's talking.
His mind busy on other things.
We hope his with joy trips on weekends,
he ends up with nothing in slings.

Now this is all meant in friendship.
In no way is hurt intended.
Speaking of special friendships,
we hope that ours is never ended.

A Rose

A single rose can say so much.
Brought to full bloom with a tender touch.
Raised and guided with heart felt care.
To wear on your party dress or in your hair.
So with this one single rose may I say?
I love you dear.
I care.

First Born of My First Born (Christy)

I was told you were expected.
That you were on your way.
Already you had started your journey,
there was nothing I could do or say.

Not happy with your mom so very young.
Unsure of this future she chose.
To bring a life into this world so hard.
What is to come in your future?
Only the Lord knows.

Maybe I didn't want to be an "old grandma".
Be young enough to enjoy my grandkids.
But oh so sad to see your mom give up her youth,
Not realizing at the time that she did.

Being a young mother is so hard.
The uphill climb can get very steep.
Tedious feedings, dirty diapers and checkups.
Sleepless nights will soon make you weep.

An early morning in autumn,
a wonderful new life arrived.
The long, long months were over,
You were the cutest, sweetest thing alive.

We a" checked you over, everything was there.
Perfect little fingers and toes.
Even a tiny smidgen of "nanas" red hair.

We did a lot of praying while you were,
on your way to us here on earth.
We even said extra prayers for mom,
to have an easy birth.

Your mom sat right up, she felt so good,
She wanted to go home right then.
Doc says she has to stay,
We can come back and see you both again.
Your dad and I left at three a.m.
With our hearts riding amongst the stars.
Twenty three miles to home,
Somehow it didn't seem that far.

Phone was ringing as we walked in.
Your mom had taken a fall.
Convulsions brought on by bleeding,
We're told as we waited and paced the hall.

It was hours before we were allowed to see her.
She was asleep, hooked up with tubes and deathly white.
Poison was all through her system.
She was in for a hell of a fight.

We stayed until she was out of danger.
It was an awful long ride home.
This ride was so different from that last one,
We both felt so very much alone.

Your dad thought I blamed him.
That your mom was so gravely ill.
I said if they both had waited,
She would be in high school still.

He built a wall against me,
I never could break it down.
Each time I tried to help you and your mom,
I would receive an angry frown.

No one is perfect in this world.
There will be times of strife.
If the love is strong and true,
Face your troubles together,
and just get on with life.

You are the first born of my first born.
I know we will disagree at times.
I will caution against breaking your heart.
Please try to do the same with mine.

Broken

What is this awful hurting thing?
Some fools call it love.
Why all the burning pain?
Where is the sunshine from above?

So very hard not to be bitter.
Would be easy to just stop trying.
Give up looking for the time of smiles.
It will never outweigh the crying.

Every cloud does have a silver lining,
Or that is what so many people say.
Why is it I cannot find it?
I have look through the night and the day.

Someday someone will come,
pick up my hurt piece by piece.
I know that when that day comes,
my heart will find release.

So Who's Complaining?

To have a big family is a wonderful thing,
Getting dressed to go out, suddenly ping.
Brother is shooting Bobbie pins,
sister pulls your hair.
You try to get even,
Bang your shin on a chair.

Reading a book while riding on a skate,
dad yells "watch the stairs".
Whoops, too late.

Try washing your hair without,
someone taking your towel.
Hitting home run, without,
baby brother yelling "foul".

Mom says "come help with these dishes,
boy if I only had three wishes.
Go to your closet for your favorite dress,
another sister got there first,
it sure is a mess.

Mom is in the doorway, says,
"you clean this room",
If I spot that sister of mine,
I'll hit her with this broom.

If I ever meet an only child,
who wants a brother, sister or two,
I'll bring them over to my house,
as I have quite a few.

Hey what the heck,
a big family is still for me.
An only child's life must be,
a lonely life indeed.

So when it comes my time,
to leave this home.
I'm really going to miss,
Mom and dad and all the rest,
who just call me sis.

Woodsy Job

For three long years I work in the woods.
Making a living as best I could.
With a twelve pound chain saw in my hands.
Proving that this domain was not just mans.

Didn't matter if trees were big or small.
To earn a living, we needed them all.
White birch, pine, maple and spruce.
Check your chain after each tree,
make sure it's not loose.

Limb out, brush up, and don't leave behind a mess.
Creatures build homes in the piles I guess.
Stack up the trailer. Take it out to the road.
Follow your tracks back in for another load.

A mountain cat followed us one day.
No matter what we did, it would not go away.
Working in winter, days were raw.
Animals were drawn be the hum of the saw.

To take a break we built a fire in the snow.
Deer and bob cats wanted to know
What had invaded their home.
They just wanted to be left alone.

Six trips I took to fill the back of the truck.
We'd take a full load the mill, with any luck.
Go home clean up run a brush through my hair.
Machine unloads it when we get there.

The work was hard, you'd need an iron back.
Break it off at two, pick the kids up at track.
Fix supper; take a nap, go to work in the mill.
Doing this day after day, I soon got my fill.

Stopped cutting trees, spent my nights with a machine.
For a number of years times were quite lean.
The kids and I would walk in the woods.
Without a chain saw. I felt so good.

When you have kids, you do what you can.
Even work in the woods cutting trees like a man.
Love them, feed them, and treat them right.
Do what needs doing and do it right.

Home for Christmas

With all the gifts and a gaily lit tree.
This is what Christmas at home, means to me.

Cheery faces and hearts filled with love.
All of God's blessings from up above.

Snow covering the lawn and trees,
children playing in it up to their knees.

Barb fusses to put a curl in her hair.
Joe's hanging mistletoe everywhere.

Christmas Eve's upon us so quick.
The kids all dream of old St' nick.

Christmas morn sure got here fast.
Whoops little John tipped over his glass.

Everyone is excited, don't want to wait.
But as always Stub and Barb are late.

Out go the lights, tree pretty and bright.
We poke and shake every gift in sight.

All the "Oh's and ah's" as you unwrap your gift.
What you see inside give your heart a lift.

Pop plays piano, everyone sings, of the love,
with God blessing and wonderful things.

Mom starts cleaning up the paper and mess.
We all pray the New Year will be,
as happy as this.

Maine, Nothing Like It

Blustering and blowing,
the pure white snow comes down.
No stars out tonight.
No shining moon to be found.
Their all hiding from sight.
The wind is so cold.
Your face gets pink and rosy.
Mittens, hat and scarf keep you warm.
But the fire inside is just plain cozy.
All seasons in Maine are beautiful.
The best of God land anywhere.
One winter away and you long to be back there.
The smell of the wood stove.
A warm shield from the storm.
No matter how far you may roam,
Maine will always be home.

Reflections of a Lost Love

Over the lush green meadows,
down to the shores of the sea.
There is a love out of the long lost past.
That keeps coming back to haunt me.

We laughed, we cried together,
whether days were dreary or sun bright.
Walked hand and hand for hours,
even when starry skies showed us it was night.

Our love kept us warm in the winter.
Made us act like children in spring.
Though we couldn't be together always,
this love we shared made our hearts sing.

We never had any children.
I have memories to keep him close by.
I cry every night in the darkness.
Oh God! Why did he have to die?

He was good kind and decent.
Our love would have had to last.
Now I must try to live for the future,
and keep his loving memory in the past.

Just a few thoughts for your hearts

At some point in our lives we all must take a good long look at what we have done and if we are really at peace and happy with every aspect of our life.

If the good Lord said you have twenty four hours before I call you home. Would you be ready?

Could you say from your heart," Yes Lord I am yours".

Could you go knowing that you have given no sadness to leave behind? My life is full. I am content.

My life is happy. I hope I have made others so.

My life is as you would want it to be.

I have made up for all the hurt I caused.

I have forgiven all those that hurt me and mine.

I have done all I could day today to be happy.

I have tried to make all those around me happy also.

I have tried to keep you in my family, Lord.

I have tried to keep you in my heart.

I thank you for all you have given me.

I thank you for always being there for me.

Even If all I wanted to do was talk.

At some point in our lives, we are all going to,

have to make this list.

A few things you will need.

Respect and curtsey for all others.

Honest heart!

Thinking and feeling.

An honest Soul to go with the heart.

Quiet time each day with you and your Lord.

Then you will see that He just really want your Faith.

Believe!

Friendship Can Mean Friendship

I don't want your heart or your money.
I need not your body or soul.
I know you've been hurt, as I have.
Or this is what I have been told.

A smile that is there when I need one.
A friendly face to send me home each work night.
To know a hand reaching out in kindness
It helps to make a work day bright.

Pay no mind when others may tease you.
Pay no mind to others may say.
I'm only asking for friendship.
Left alone we'll have it one day.

I am bad tempered, loud and boastful.
This I do not intend to amend.
But I'm also something that everyone needs.
A friend when a friend needs a friend.

My One Day of Rest

I work away from home six nights out of a week.
I'm so done in and so pooped out I can hardly speak.
This is my account of it at its very best,
an account of that seventh day,
my day of rest.

Home from work at seven a.m.
My work's week is supposed to be done.
A loud noise from over my head,
tells me my family's day has just begun.

Cora wouldn't mind last night.
Brenda just had to sass.
Helena and Corleen fighting over a drink,
chalk up a broken glass.

Lori is sulking over who sits in
my rocking chair.
Janetta still hogging the bathroom,
she has to finish washing her hair.

Sherry forgot again
to put up dads lunch.
He thinks it's done on purpose,
but then it's just a hunch.

Wendy is still upstairs.
The music is a blaring.
The house is such a mess,
though she is far from caring.

Mom! You going to the store today?
Mom! Can we go outside to play?
There's dishes to do, lunch to get.
A couple more hours I'll get to bed yet.

It's that time of day to break up the first spat.
Knock it off you guys, I won't stand for that.
Clothes in the washer, then out of the dryer.
I ask for a little help, the T.V volume goes higher.
Father is pouting.
Something is wrong.
I would ask "what's the matter?"
But answer would be too long.

Lunch time is here.
breakfast isn't even digested;
and as I think of it,
I haven't rested.

A coffee at this time,
sure would taste good.
Dad gets into his head,
it's time to chop the wood.

Some go with him.
Some go outside to play.
An me, ah huh!
In bed for the day.

Then comes a yell "company",
So up I get and dress,
Just to hear Judy say,
"Boy are you a mess."

Drink more coffee and chit chat,
Just for an hour or two.
Then up she gets, out she goes,
with an "I'll see you".

Well as long as I am up,
on this my day of rest,
I may as well get dinner started,
and visit with a bunch that is the best,
my family.

A Life full of Dreams

What good has your life been?
If all you have done is dream.
Some place all their wishes on the stars.
Saying I'd like to do this or that.
But they just keep walking and talking,
Listening to others chit chat.
Our lives are but a hand full of clay,
To mold as we will.
Your back is for more than to just lean upon,
Let it weaken and you will never walk proud.
Make your own path in life.
Walk it proudly and free.
No one person is free of sin.
It need not bring you to your knees,
Accept to Him.
Feel not sorry for yourself.
If you are surrounded by stardust and dreams.
Go ahead, gaze at the heavens,
But keep a prayer in your heart.
Don't leave all the answers Sitting out there,
Waiting for you to find them to make your dreams come true.
Find them and fight for them,
If what you want be true.
Take the stars out of the skies.

Put that sparkle in someone's eyes,
It shines brighter.
Take your dreams and share them.
They become truer.
At the end of your time here,
Will you be proud to say?
I have done what I was put here to do.
Just what good has your life been?
If all you have done is dream.
"No good, No good all!
Work hard to make all the dreams you can come true.
Along the way some of yours will to.

Love is a Dream

You say I'm your dream girl.
The apple of your eye.
But as I sit here writing this,
I know we must say goodbye.

You sometimes say the nicest things,
A girl could want to hear.
You caress me with the sweetest words,
It's music to my ears.

We both belong to others,
To them we must be true.
If we could live our lives over,
I'd choose to love only you.

You tell me, I'm in all your dreams,
So that you never want to wake.
But you know we must be true them,
Or it's their hearts we break.

I have promised to love, honor and obey.
You made this promise too.
If you could hurt someone else like that
I wouldn't love you as I do.

How do we keep the hurt from,
Showing in our eyes?
How do we replace the tears,
with stars from the skies?

But even when the skies are cloudy,
my sunshine in life is you.
How can we feel so happy,
then suddenly feel so blue?

We both belong to others.
To them we must be true.
If we could but live our lives over,
my only love in life would be you.

So go on with your life, my dear one.
The hurt will pass with time.
I know I will be in your heart forever.
As you will always be in mine.

What I've learned about life

Ask a man to not do something,
he thinks you're trying to tie him down.
Tell him to do as he pleases,
he thinks you do not care for him.
Baby him; he wants to be treated like a man.
Treat him like a grown man.
He wants to be treated like your special baby.
Kiss him, he doesn't want you too.
Don't kiss him and he thinks you don't want to.
Give him advice, your nagging.
Don't offer it, is when he wants you input.
Love him; he doesn't think you love him enough.
Show angry he claims he's done nothing wrong.
What is a woman to do?
Baby him without taking any of the manliness from him.
Choose your words with care when giving advice.
Care for him without hanging him with that gold band.
Love him just right.
Kiss him just enough.
Above all stay true and be his and his alone.

Happiness?

Happiness is a word called love; let's see if I can describe it.
It's special looks, joy and tears, if real you cannot hide it.
Giving birth to a child, the greatest joy, by far.
Building a new home or buying a car.
Saying you're sorry when you know you're not wrong,
Creating a world where you both can be strong.
From the time you are fresh faced, till there is gray in your hair.
When your children have grown, gone out on their own,
You'll have just each other but never feel alone.
When you still hold hands after fifty years,
Just thinking back brings thankful tears,
Your own true love has withstood every test,
You have lived a fulfilling life,
You have been blessed.

Corner of My Heart

Of all the people in my world you,
are my favorite one.
Of all the sunsets in the sky.
you're my setting sun.
I love you for what you are.
Not what you can do for me.
You'll be in my heart,
till the salt melts from the sea.
The moon in its season, is many,
shapes and size.
These feelings that I have,
are deeper than you realize.
How often have I told you?
I try honestly to be fair.
How else can I show you?
That I really and truly care.
You're bitter, wounded and so hurt.
From a love that was untrue.
Look beyond your angry to us.
I didn't cause this hurt in you.
We have a union now.
Surely blessed from above.
Don't let something from the past,
put a shadow on our love.
I know no way to tell you.
No other way to say.
You're my moon and my sunshine.
I'm yours in every way.

More reflections from long ago

As I sit here alone late at night. I can't help but reflect
Upon the past nineteen or so years.
I ask myself just where all this time has gone?
Why does it seem they have gone so fast?
As I think back I am honest enough to say,
I do have a few regrets.
Who are we? You and I, Where did we come from?
We have had our times.
Some good. Some not good at all.
Me all mixed up and bitter.
Fed up with an abusive x mate.
You so angry at life, trying to forget a cheating x wife.
Your kids didn't like me.
I didn't like their snotty ways.
Feelings were hurt, love was misplaced.
Angry and mistrust soon took its place.
I didn't cook from opening a can.
I fixed food from beginning to end.
I knew how to cook.
I knew how to clean.
I could do things they had never seen.
I baked homemade pies.
I swept and moped the floors.
I even found lost socks behind closed doors.
We pushed and we shoved and
We learned to tolerate.

We worked and we tried to build a family.
We learned that some things in life are just not to be.
Four of our girls went their separate ways.
The youngest son went straight to hell.
I guess that's where he stayed.
The older son played it smart.
He joined the Air Force and got away.
So here we were just you and me trying to make a life.
At this end of nineteen years you're no husband
And I'm still no one's wife.
We have to just wait and see where it all goes.

A Racers Heart

Delia Cody is her name.
Driving her way to glory and fame.
Behind the wheel, she's hard to pass.
Second division, but really first class.
A lady in slacks. A lady in a dress.
Always worried her hairs a mess.
"028" is painted on her car.
Just watch, these two are going to go far.
Her pit crew is right on the ball.
Without them, she wouldn't be there at all.
The only woman stock driver near or far.
She drives against men with a hell of a car.
The roar of the crowd is music to her ears.
She and that car deserve every cheer.
This year's season is near to a close.
It's really going to bore her just powdering her nose.
There's another big race coming next year.
So Dee, sit back, relax and have a cold beer.

Woolen Mill Mouse

As much as I really hate to admit it.
When I go to work its dark and its night.
In the corner on the wall of this old mill.
There is this wee shadow of light.

At three a.m. and I am resting.
It's my lunch break from work you see!
In that scarcely lit corner, there he sits.
He stays there peeking up at me.

Most women would holler or scream.
But I think he's really sweet.
Not four inches long from his,
little black nose to his tiny furry feet.

He dashes all around this dirty ole mill.
Though it's way too big for his house.
By now you all must know I'm talking about,
a real cute little fuzzy brown mouse.

Tossing bit of bread crumbs to lure him.
He doesn't know I just want to be his friend . . .
If he keeps getting in the way of the big bosses
Then he's going to meet an early end.

One night by the spinners I cornered him
Just wanted to give him a little pat.
His look seems to say as he glared up at me.
"I have a big brother they call rat"

I found him one night as I came to break late.
I knew by the look of him,
The poor thing had,
once too often tempted fate.

Badly hurt and bleeding.
He was in terrible pain.
My three a.m. buddy died at one o'clock.
Never to be my friend again.

I did miss him in the weeks that followed.
My coworkers called me a sentimental fool.
But if you had lost the only trusted friend you had,
would you not be unhappy and lonesome to?

God's creatures can be trusted.
Ease your life if you let them and make you smile.
I will seem to forget him someday.
The memories will be there for a long, long while.

My little friend, the woolen mill mouse.

What to Change

I don't wish to be rich nor famous.
I don't care to be known worldwide.
I just want people I care about,
To know the life I've never tried to hide.

Sometimes I look back and I wonder.
What I would change if I could.
I would do the same, I guess.
For we must take the bad with the good.

Not a day I'd give back of my life time.
Though some are remembered with regret.
Should I live to a hundred and two,
I have a lot to learning to do yet.

I have seen new ways, I've tried them.
I have made mistakes and learned from them.
I do enjoy and like most everyone I meet.
Accept me on equal terms. Don't grovel at my feet.

I've done a little traveling.
But my heart has stayed close to home.
I am content and happy now.
I have no urge to roam.

I have a family that shows their love.
My true friends accept my many ways.
When I'm down and sad they cheer me.
They make me laugh throughout my days.

Sure I have a few regrets.
But the good outweighs the bad.
Being raised poor as we were,
I'm thankful for the life that I've had.

What would I change if I could?
Nothing, nothing at all.

So Much Power

Softly the breeze blew.
Rain drops came gently down.
The river flowed every on,
but it was raising
every so slowly
to the top of its banks.
Water came high and brown
taking everything in its path.
Leaving tears and heartache
as it tears up the earth around.
Homes and lives go down stream.
Their life's work becomes just a dream.
The rains came, washed it away.
Took the barn and house that day.
Didn't know it could be that strong.
One minute here next second gone.
The river made a new path that day,
It even took the land away.
No land to build on,
No youth to start anew.
New laws to tell us,
What we can and cannot do.
The rivers still flowing,
everything a total lose.
We thought we had our lives under control.
little did we know.
The gentle rain and sweet breeze
grow much stronger
Because it let God take it in hand.
Taking back the earth,
Being destroyed by man.

Hands of Grace

The eyes of despair,
the hands of grace.
The sorrowful look,
upon her face

Long worked finger,
bony and thin.
So close to tears,
that quivering chin.

Embracing his sad lady,
to ease tears as they flow.
That hollow look on his face,
"now where do we go"?

What will we do?
everything is gone.
Could we salvage something,
so to just carry on?

The sadness of losing,
all that you own.
The utter grief of,
losing your home.

Mementos gone,
the heartfelt wrench.
That terrible smell,
the awful stench.

But those hands are there,
to start a new.
For she has his love,
thank God he has hers too.

I Miss You

I miss you since you went away.
Think of you more often than words can say.
I still see you standing there.
With that special smile upon your face.
I thank God for so peacefully taking you,
into His loving embrace.
How we laughed and joked with each other,
on your last day.
Then within a single hour,
you quickly went away.
From Heaven you have guided me,
as you have always done.
So while other kids may have grandpas,
You "gump" were my only one.

Love you, miss you.
"Spike"

Always "Pop" to Me

Why is that there days I miss you more than others?
Why after all this time I'm still sad and blue?
I know why I'm angry pop.
I didn't get chance to say good bye and I love you.

I was to come not to visit, but to bring you back.
They said you're well enough to come home.
I retired early, so not tire on the trip.
Then we got the call, it was a fatal heart attack.

My head would not believe it.
My heart was broken in two.
I was so angry that you were taken away.
I didn't even get a chance to hug you.

Mom stopped coming to our house,
after you went away.
We would go down to see her.
She never had much to say.

She would talk about her garden.
Tell me stories of her neighbors and such.
Didn't ask how I was doing.
It was like she didn't care that much.

You are with me every day pop.
Everywhere I go.
I still sit alone and talk to you.
When I'm down and low.

The stories you used to tell me.
The laughter we always shared.
The many little things you did,
To show me that you cared.

The memories will have to do, pop.
It's all I have left of you.
Love for all that we shared and,
of the pictures I have but few.

I laugh as I sit writing of you.
I shed a tear or two.
I'll always laugh when I think of our time together.
I still cry because I'll always miss you.

I'll look for the signs that you're near pop.
Be it the road runner, cardinal or chickadee.
Whenever I see even a blue jay,
I'll know your sending your love down to me.

Love you.

Three Wishes

In the misguided days of lost youth.
One forever searches for lost truth.

Painted faces made up like happy clowns.
But tears wash away the paint to painful frowns.

Where are the trusted friends, the helping hands?
Why does cheating and hurting come so easily to man?

If three wishes I could but ask.
Universal peace would be the first task.

Freedom from sickness, hunger for all mankind.
Enough of the needed things would also be fine.

But . . . from all this only one wish could be had.
It would be, I could have known and loved you better . . .
Dad.

Memories

In a home so full, but empty.
The whole bunch gone different ways.
It gives me a chance to reflect and write,
Of long past bygone days.
Remember when they were little?
With tiny bruised elbows and knees.
When all there seemed to be needed,
Was a hug or a kiss to please?
Now! One is so unhappy in a marriage.
One out school very soon.
Both trying so hard to grow.
Another with a small baby,
And dissatisfied with life.
My own baby, sixteen this year.
Ahead and behind her time.
Two sons have also come my way.
Good boys when they try to be.
It sometimes shows through though
They're a little resentful of me.
They came into my life half grown.
When their mother walks out and left.
Their father and I are together.
We plan and hope and we worry.
Just what will their lives be?
Will they use the guidelines we gave them?
Will they listen to him and to me?
How any child turns out today,
In this so troubled world, is a light or heartache.
We can only pray and keep the faith
of our love open to them.
With luck that will show them
the rest of the way to a good life.

My Twilight Years

May I never forget the strength that
comforted me,
in the many darkened hours of the past.

Spare me from bitterness and sharp passions
of unguarded moments.

May I not forget that poverty and riches,
are of the mind and spirit,
not of the heart.

May my thoughts and actions keep me
forever true to myself.

Let me not follow the clamor
of this lost world.

But lets me walk calmly down
my own path.

Give me a few friends who love me
for who I am.

Keep ever burning before my tired eyes,
the kindly lights of hope.

Though age and infirmity overtake me,
and I come not within sight,
of the castle of my dreams.

Teach me still to be thankful for life,
and it's sweet memories.

May the evening's twilight,
find me gentle still,
in the twilight of my years.

Faded Youth

In the sudden realization of lost youth.
Looking back to seek only truth.

When looking back brings only regret.
Keep in mind you've not seen the best yet.

Remember when you were just a kid?
You weren't ready yet, so you hid.

You played your games till the last roar.
Show up soon though or your butt would be sore.

To tease your brothers was always so neat.
To see them more often now would be a treat.

Life sometimes has cruel ways,
Of making us grateful for our younger days.

Growing up takes its time, to make us aware.
Our yesterdays and youth are no longer there.

Life has its pleasures. Some quite profound.
Looking and seeing loved ones all around.

A walk in the meadow, Stroll through the park.
The sweet wind song of the soulful lark.

In today's world it's hard to be good.
Harder still to do as you know you should.

Too many world crises, too many sick heads.
So many temptations. Too many tears shed.

Ole "Huck" and his raft are gone sure enough
To live in today's world you need to be tough

Just be free and easy, do as you please.
Hell! "coke" is no problem. I can beat it with ease.

Now folks don't you worry, if you think 'booze' is a must.
A call in the late night, it's your child's first 'bust'.

The years of struggle, frustration and fret.
Peace of mind, less worry is so hard to get.

You know it is in them. You wait for that special sign.
You pray that you'll be here to see them walk that straight line

They can make you so happy, also sometimes sad.
Lift you up one day, next day make you so mad.

Lord what has happened to their life's spirit?
Did a warning bell sound? Did they not hear it?

Be honest with the world, but first in their heart
Facing themselves with the truth is just a start.

It is so hard to let go of your youth.
Lord please guide them to find that truth.

He Thinks I Have a Cheaters Heart
(After Thirty three years)

All these thoughts tumble through my mind.
To a different place and different time.
Where hurt can no longer touch me.
Where my heart cannot be shattered.
Where once my life meant something.
What did I do? When did it all start?
When did he first think? She's a cheat with no heart!
That I would do to him what she had done.
Over thirty years it did no good to be true.
I still got the blame while she runs.
He didn't even see that what he thought wasn't me.
I was never a cheater and never would be.
My whole world crashed that day.
May as well have had a strong wind just blow it away.
I cried in my car, as I drove away from home.
I cried in my room at night on my own.
Even as a child I never felt so hurt or alone.
After a while I had to move on.
I couldn't be happy nor would I pretend.
I couldn't talk to him without being sharp.
He'd enter a room I would have to leave.
I needed a little time and space to grieve.
My heart and life as I knew it had died.
Nothing meant anything to me anymore.
I even sought help to show me how to forgive.

The ache will be in my heart,
For however long I may live.
The thing I find most hurtful,
The one thing I cannot get by.
He told my child instead of me.
To realize that after all this time we spent,
building a life he doesn't know me as I am.
I have wasted thirty years of my life.
I am angry.
I will go on doing my part in life and this marriage.
I will try to put what is left of my heart into it.
I am lost now.
I do not know what to do but work, cook and clean.
Take it one day at a time.
Never take your happiness for what it seems.
A couple of words can take away all your dreams.
You think you know someone you love.
Think again.

These particular words were put to paper when I had come from a wake for an old and dear friend. I had known this friend for over fifty five years. I knew her dreams. Her want to do's in life. I realized that except for her children, she lost all her other hopes for herself and what she wanted to do with her life.

I guess I'm filling one of my dreams now by remembering all these things and putting them into this book for my family, friends and anyone that I have met along the way, hoping that if you read the words to the verse and feel you have not for filled your life dreams and hopes you will start. NOW!

Wasted Time

I guess I'm rather spoiled.
In an unselfish way.
I want my friends to be forever,
sometimes they have to go away.

I really like the little things.
Tiny birds up in the trees.
A sunset from a distance hill,
it takes so little to please.

A bubbling brook so clear,
you can see the fish swim by.
Maybe a lake so calm,
you can see clouds drift lazily in the sky.

A walk by that lake.
A day in the park.
The sun on my face,
star gazing after dark.

I don't want to live forever.
I would like my health to stay.
Sometimes I'd give most anything,
To have a pain free day.

Yes, I'm spoiled and just a little sad.
Neither time nor money,
will bring back the youth we had.

It's not the age that bothers.
It's the time that passing by.
Time that is so wasted.
Time now lost to you and I.

Take time now just for time's sake.
It will not stand still,
take it before it's too late.

For all the times we've said,
"Oh just let it lie".
Don't look now but your future,
Just told you bye, bye.

It came, it went.
It will be completely gone soon.
To wish for any of your time back,
is like howling at the moon.

Not much good at all.

The Biopsy

The trials of life are really small.
You reach a point where you think
You've faced them all.

It's a simple test, so they say.
It's just a little bump
but it won't go away.

Go sign in. Please take seat.
Try to read and relax,
Your name is called;
you jump to your feet.

Why do they ask,
"how are you"? Nobody knows!
You break into a sweat,
Nurse says "take off your clothes".

Lay down on your stomach,
which is sometimes hard to do.
Two holes in the table,
to put your breast through.

The probing and poking,
the machine starts going.
Two hours of testing,
two weeks of not knowing.

Now it's the fear and the wait.
Trying to live normal,
was the test too late?

You get that call on the phone.
It needs to come out,
be assured you're not alone.

As you face the knife.
Then you can thank God
for being in your life.

It's over; it's done just a little sore.
With the love that's all around me,
I'm not fearful anymore.

It took a full year for
For me to write this down.
There is one special thing,
I have found,
I am loved.

Why

Why is it so hard, to have faith in the world today?
So much hate and anger.
Where did all the love go anyway?
Try to look for good.
I was always told.
I have tried to find good all my life.
Now I just feel too old.
When did we become a "to hell with you "world?
God did not plan it this way.
If He were here in person, walking amount us today.
Would anybody Liston or just laugh and walk away.
Before you do something that is going to hurt someone.
Think to yourself "would I like it if this
happened to someone I love?"
Reach out your hand to help, not hurt.
Reach to help someone up, not to knock them down.
I try very hard to be happy, to make people around me happy too.
The back stabbing and the whispers some people can't seem to live without,
makes the world an unhappy place and that is so sad, but true.
Why is it that a heart that feels so full of sadness?
Feels like a big empty hole in ones chest.
Why is the body so very tired?
When will the tired mind get some rest?

God is Watching

What God created was a beautiful place.
What it is today is a slap to His face.
What He started as a glorious plan,
Is being destroyed day after day, by man.

The greed for power and money is the
cause of His strife.
The lies and the cheating
is just a way of life.

The wars of years past.
The wars in the world today.
The many prayers of the innocent.
To just take the hate away.

The eruptions of mountains.
Planes fall from the sky.
Unexplained floods and droughts.
Do you ever ask yourself why?

We take His skies His stars and moon.
We take for granted the sun up above.
We destroy the forest He gave us.
What we take from Him in greed,
He could take it back soon.

He gave His only son to cleanse this land.
He could get tired of holding out His hand.
It's about time to start giving back.
Time to say you're sorry for getting off track.

You don't have to give up your whole life style.
Be honest and true to others for a while.
Give up looking out just for yourself would be a start.
Show Him that you do care.
But show Him with your heart.

He is watching us all.

Maddy's Wondering Thoughts

Wouldn't it be surreal to live in a world where people really were nice to each other all the time?

Why are people always looking for what they don't have? Why not enjoy the life you were given?

Sadness has a way of sneaking into your head and then your heart to make the days seem really long and the nights ever so lonely.

Where is the shoulder for you when you have a need to just let go and cry?

Sometimes you hurt so bad on the inside that it is an everyday battle to not hurt those you care about. It is hard to keep the angry from striking at those that mean the most in this world to you.

When you try all your life to do the right thing and still get crap for living.

It is such a sad thing to live with the knowing that I wasted thirty years of my life.

Being true and was thought to be a cheater anyway.

I was always blamed for things that I didn't do as I grew up.

I really thought that as I grew my life would speak for itself.

Guess some things never do change.

Addendum